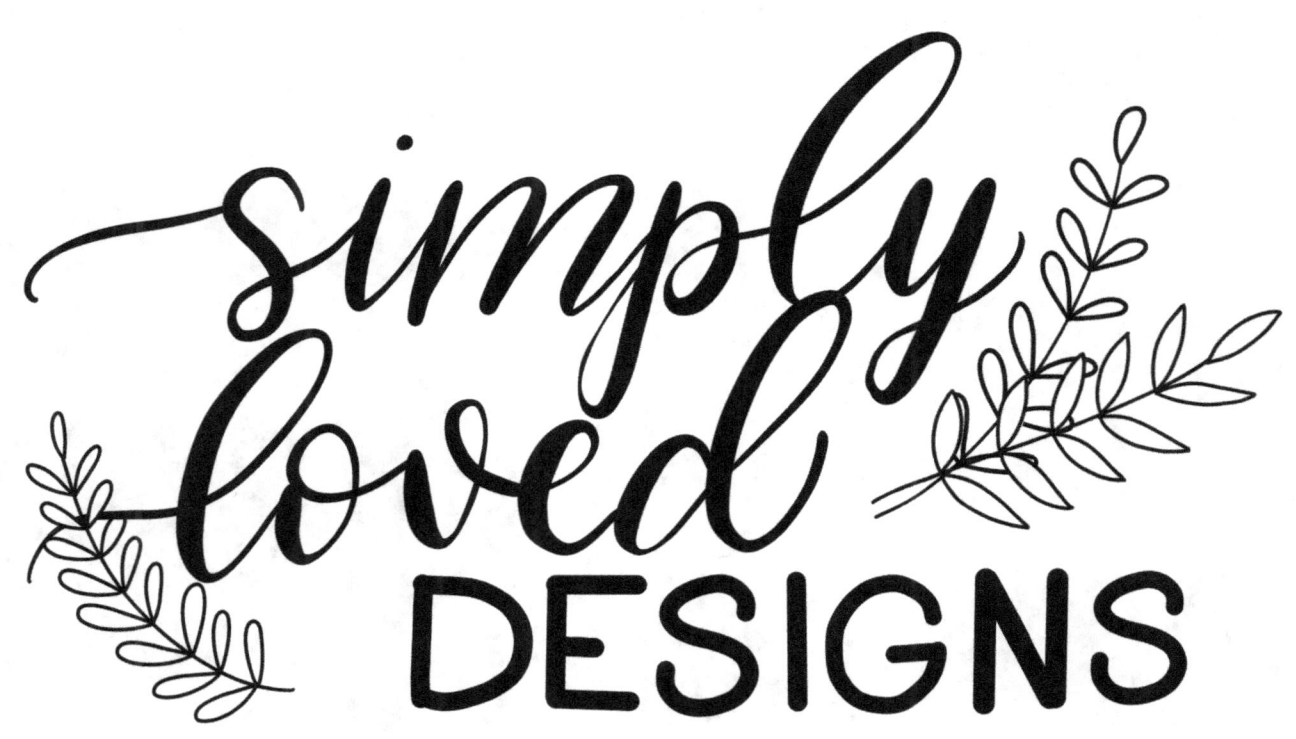

CHRISTMAS HYMNS: A COLORING BOOK
© JULIA TAYLOR MILLAR OF SIMPLY LOVED DESIGNS

THIS BOOK BELONGS TO:

_____

JOY TO THE WORLD

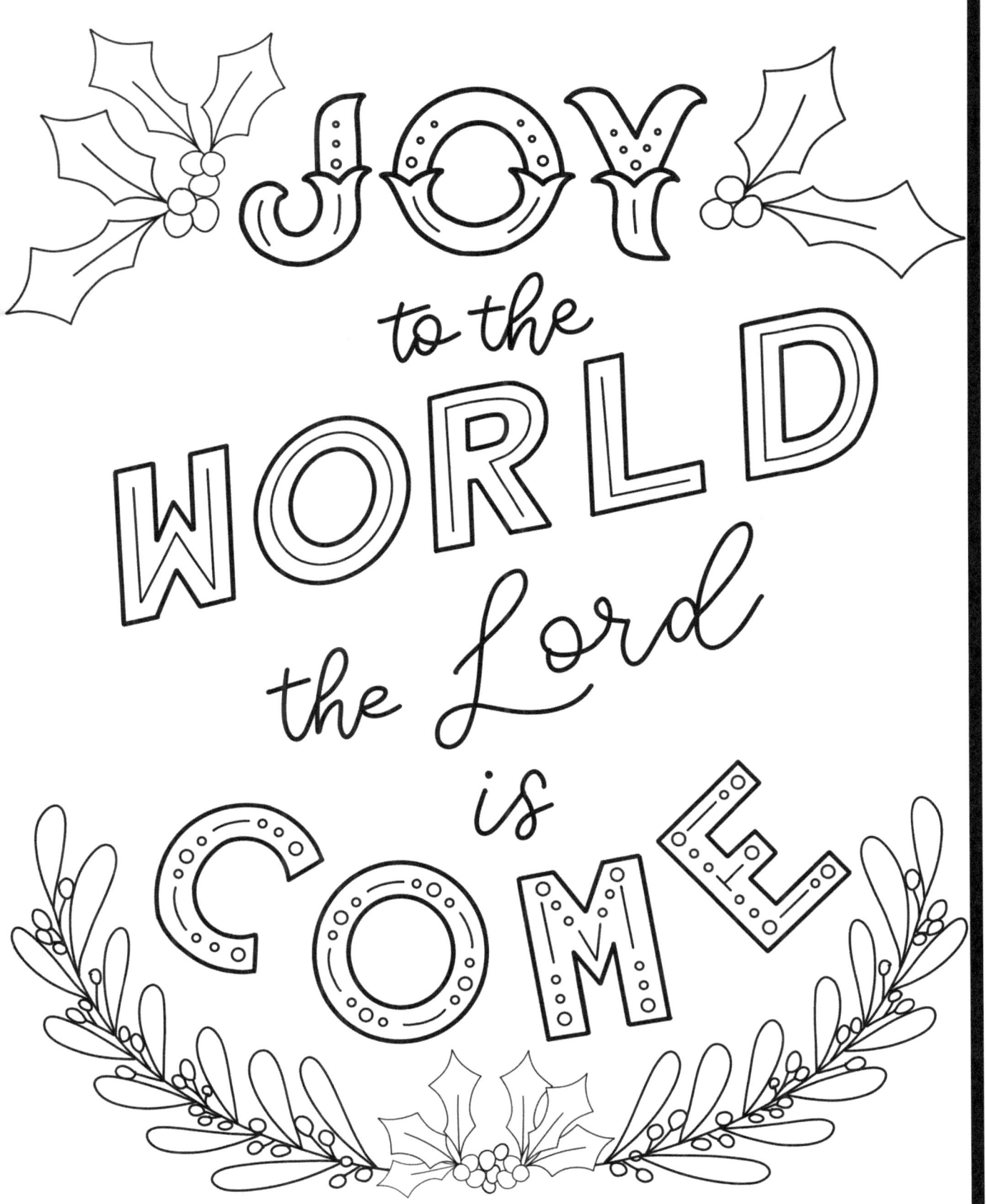

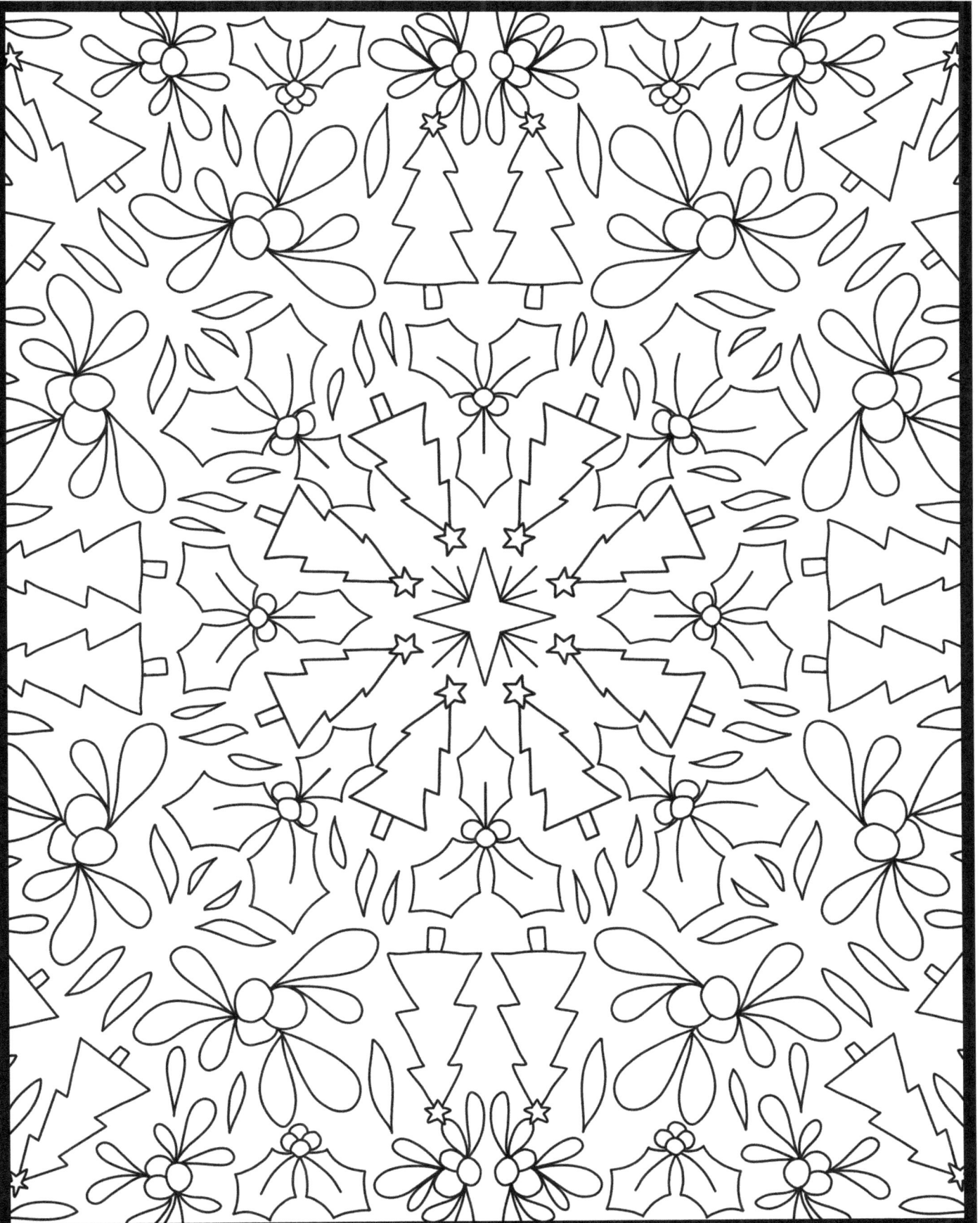

OH, COME ALL YE FAITHFUL

Yea, LORD we greet thee BORN this happy MORNING

ONCE IN ROYAL DAVID'S CITY

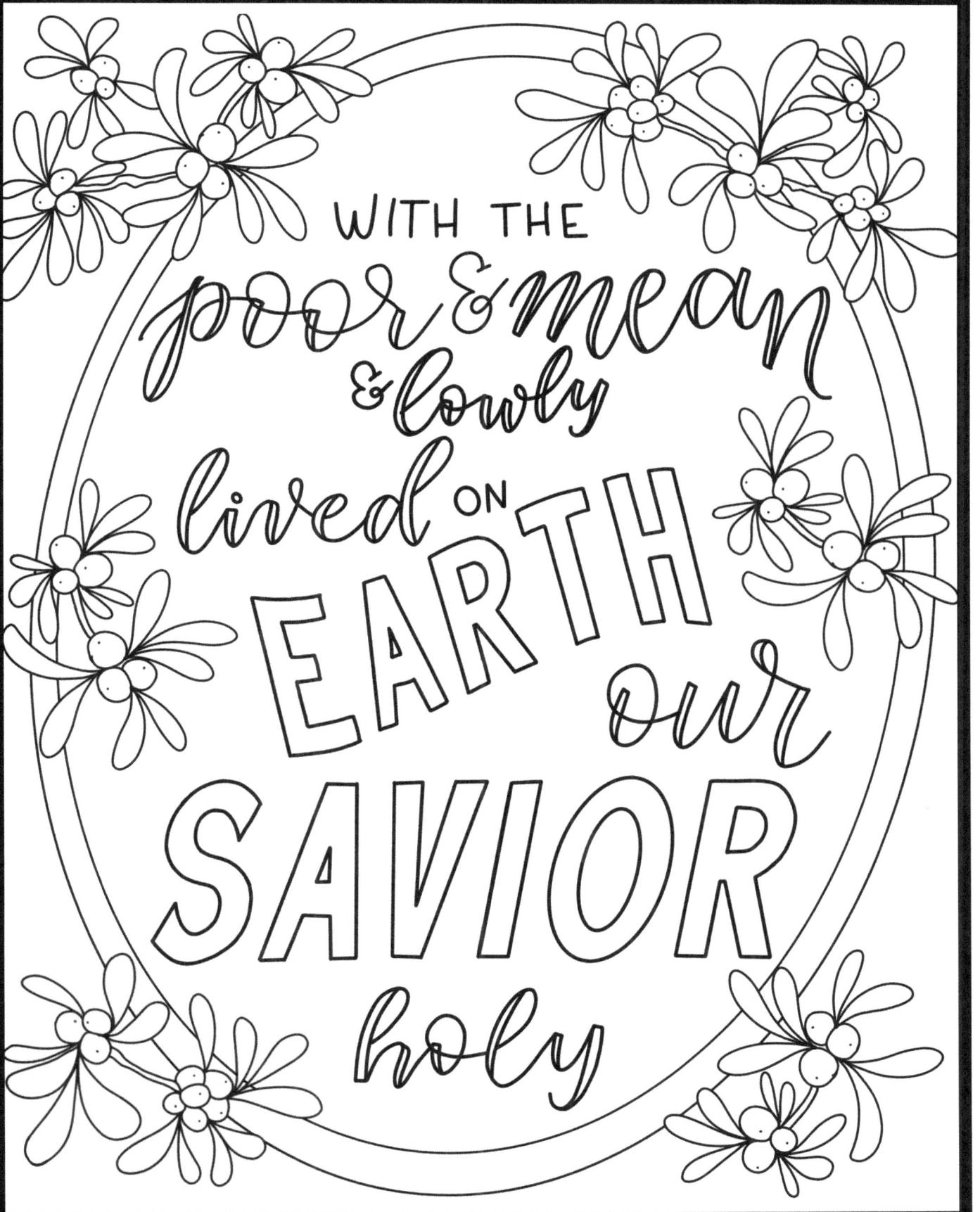

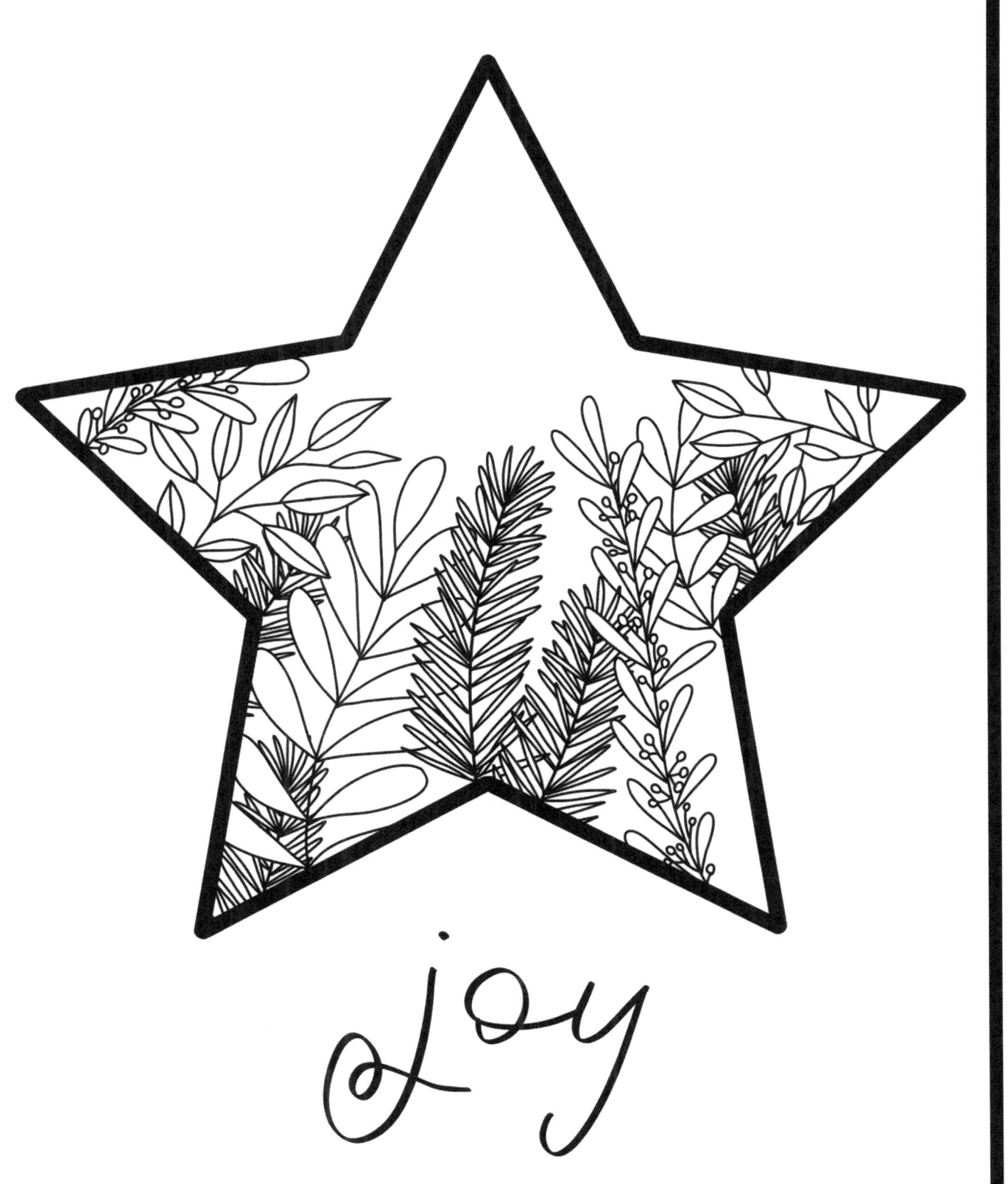

GOD REST YE MERRY GENTLEMEN

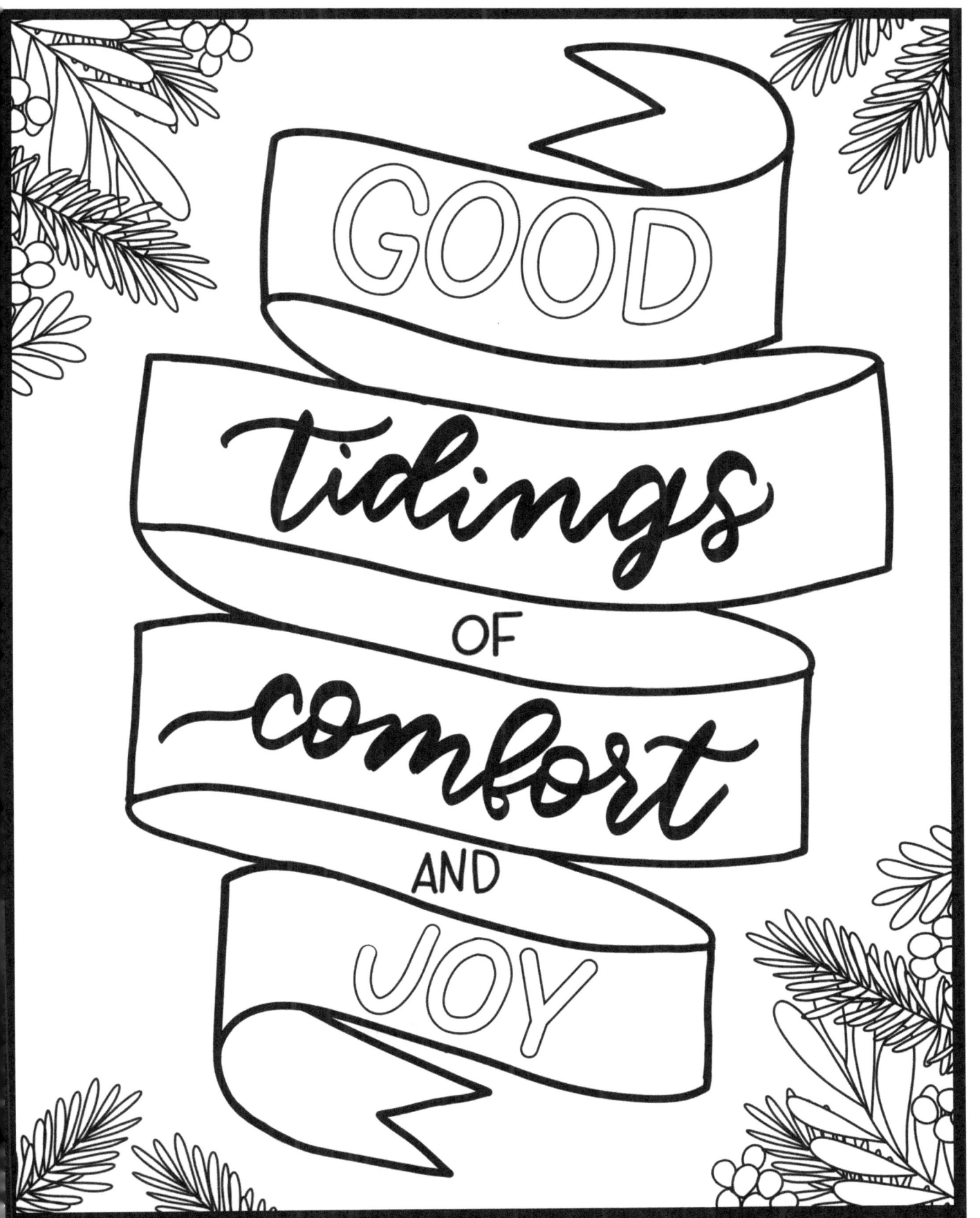

AWAY IN A MANGER

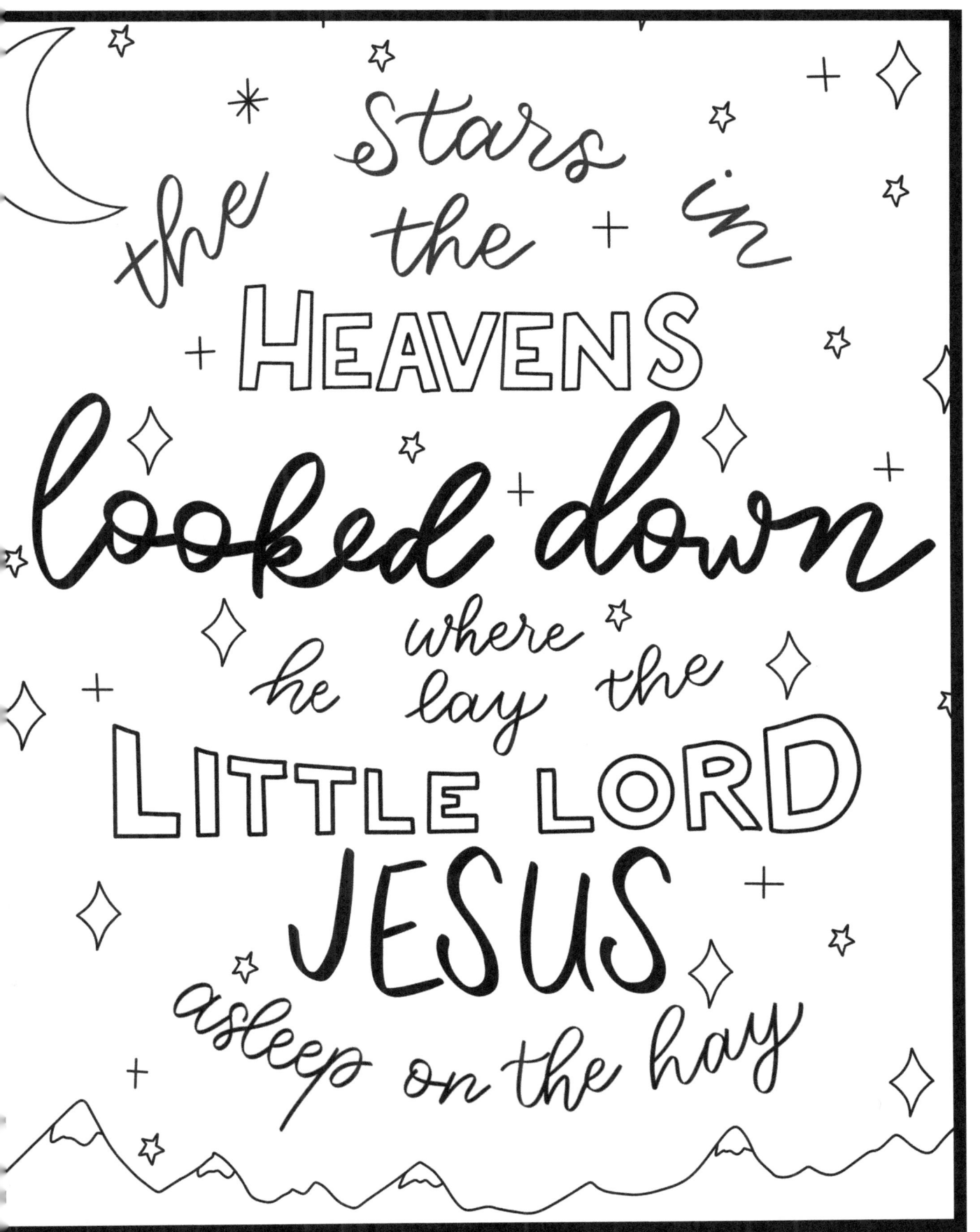

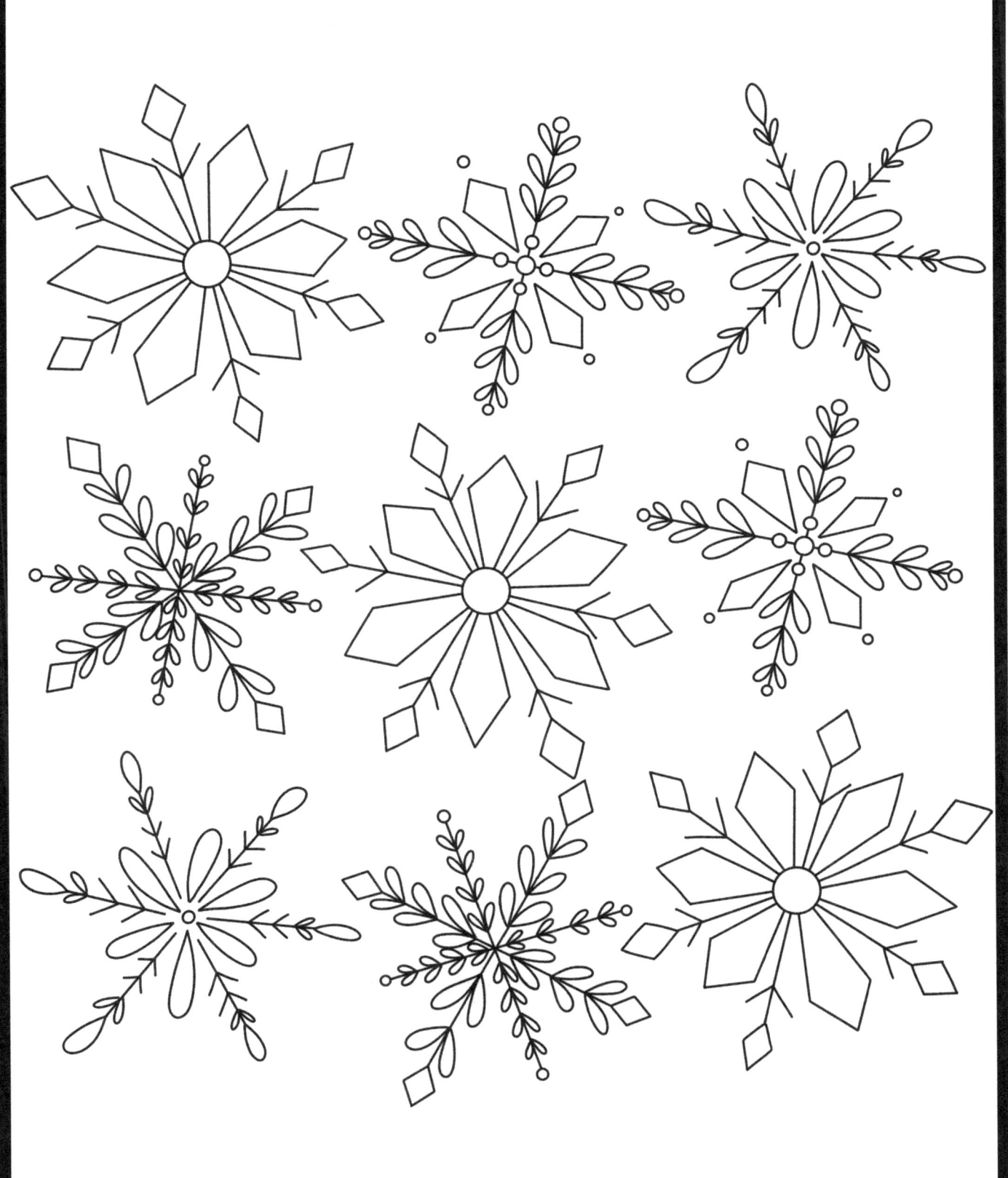

THE FIRST NOEL

NOEL
born is the KING of Israel

O LITTLE TOWN OF BETHLEHEM

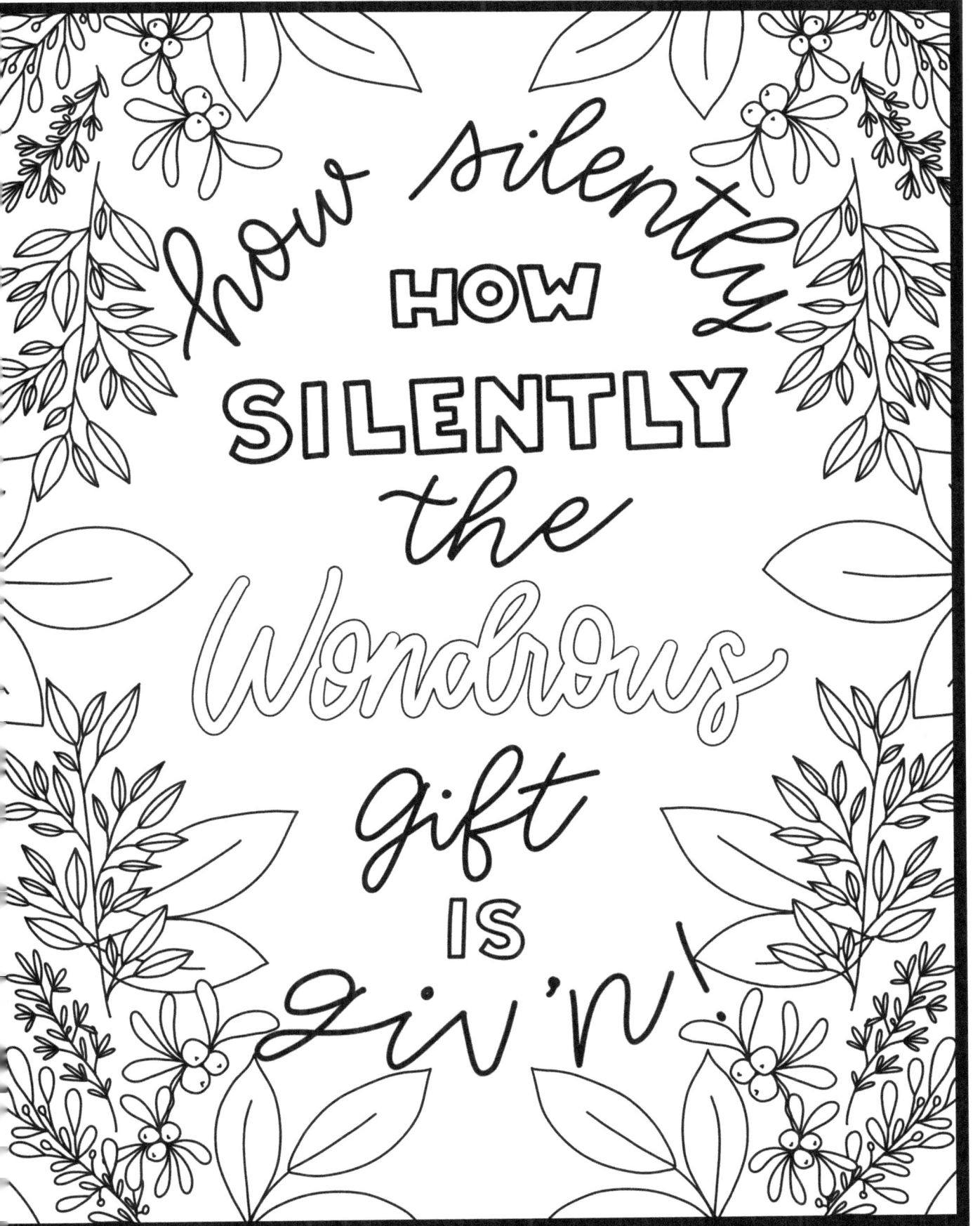

WHILE SHEPHERDS WATCHED THEIR FLOCKS

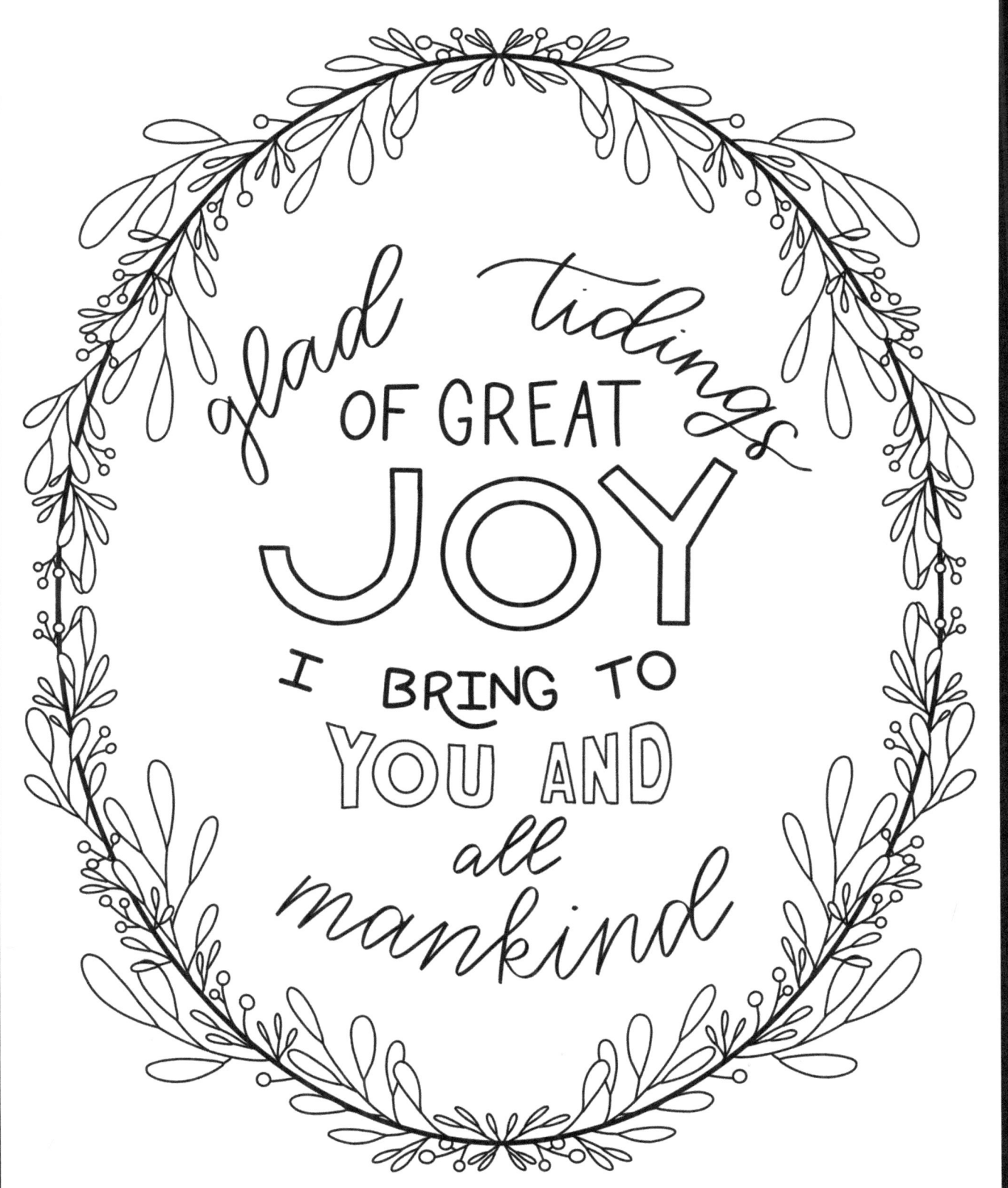

FAR, FAR AWAY ON JUDEA'S PLAINS

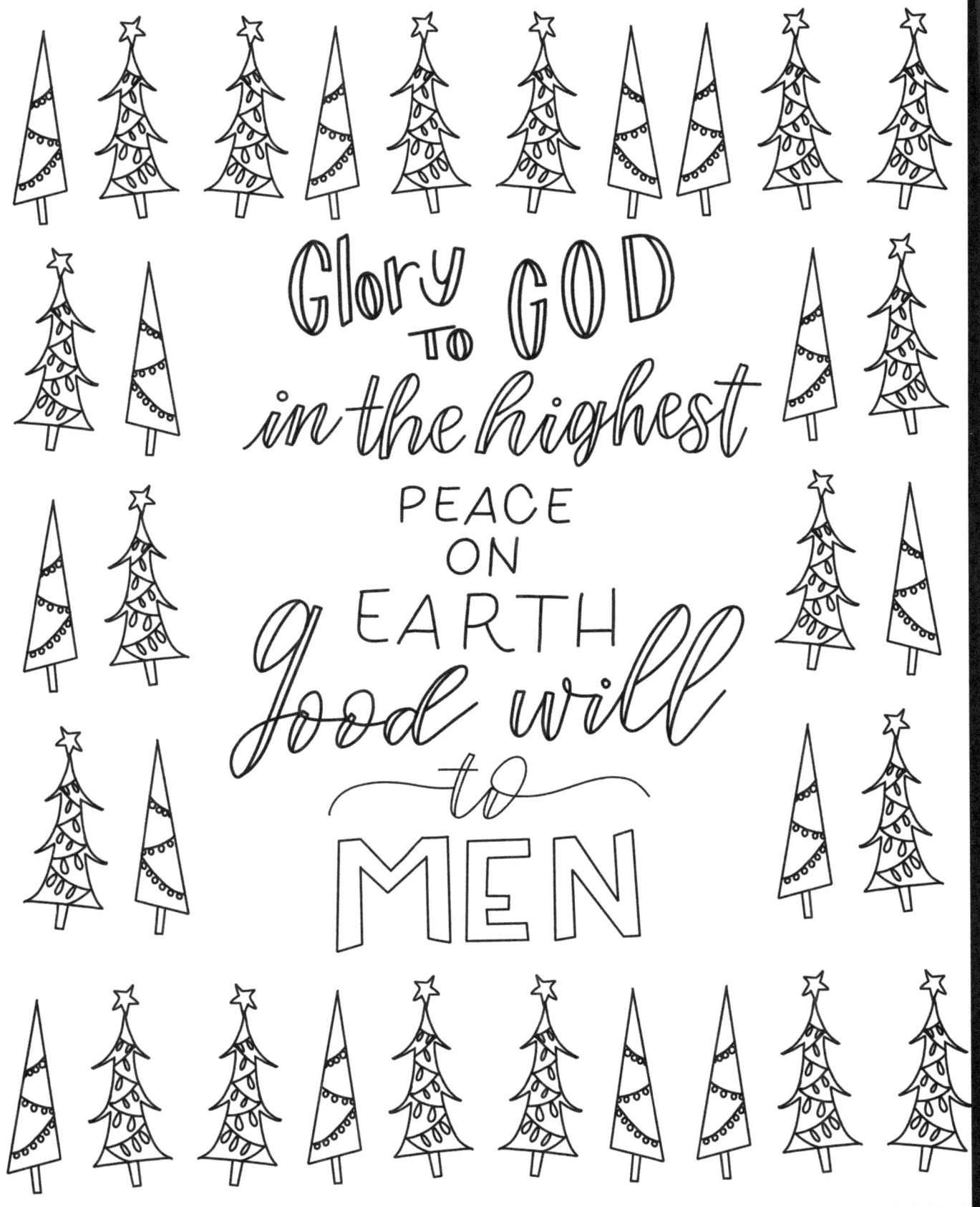

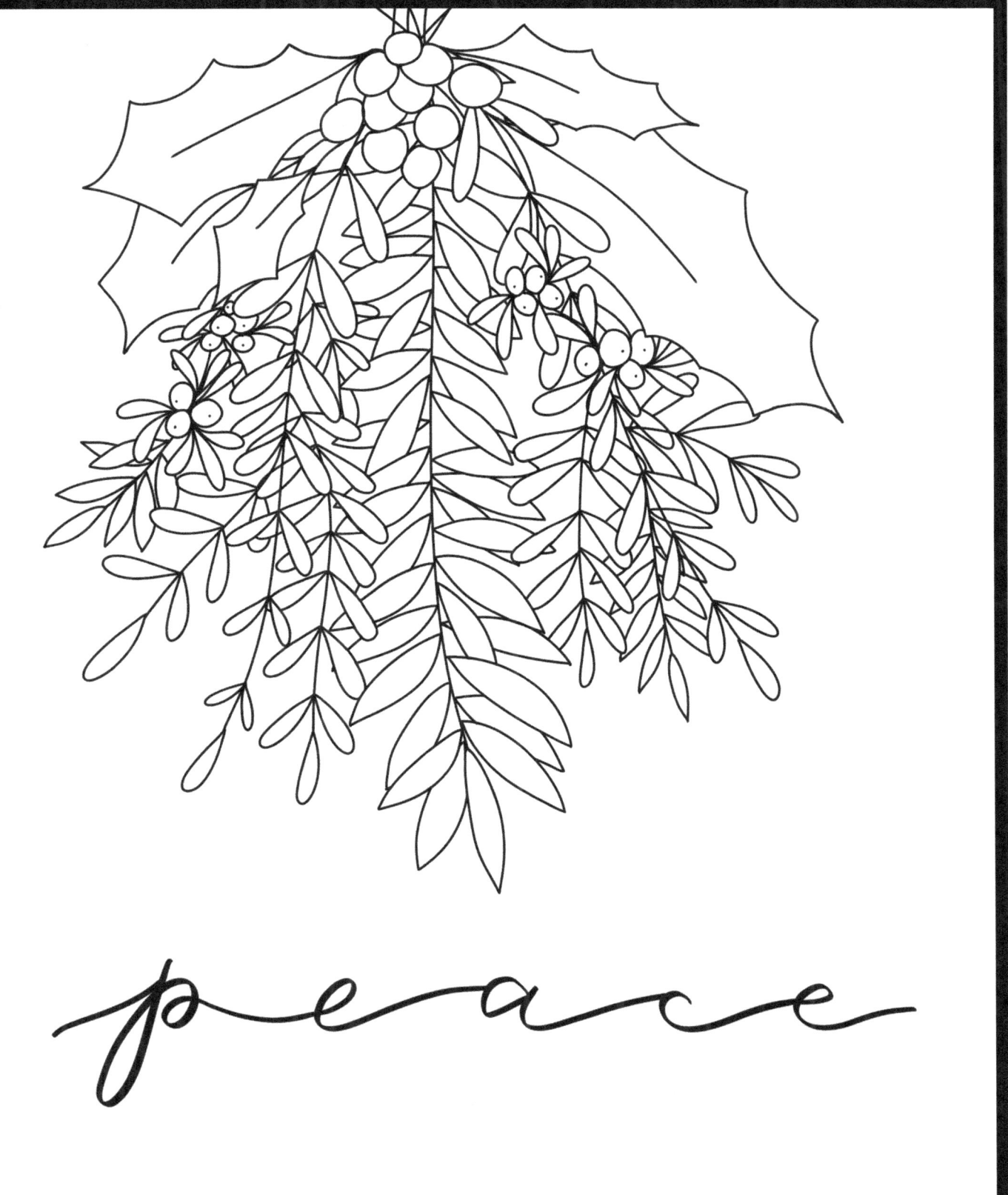

I HEARD THE BELLS ON CHRISTMAS DAY

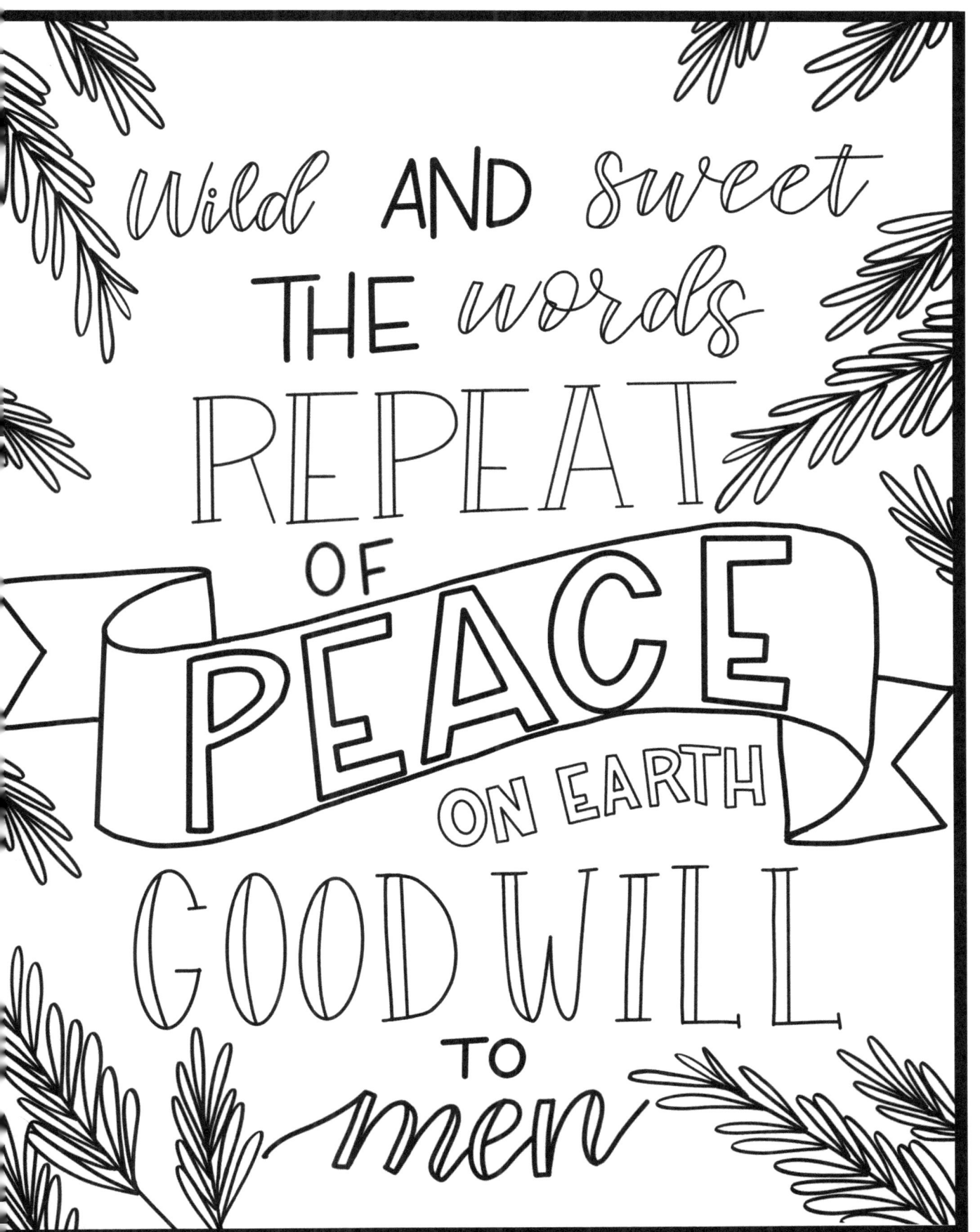

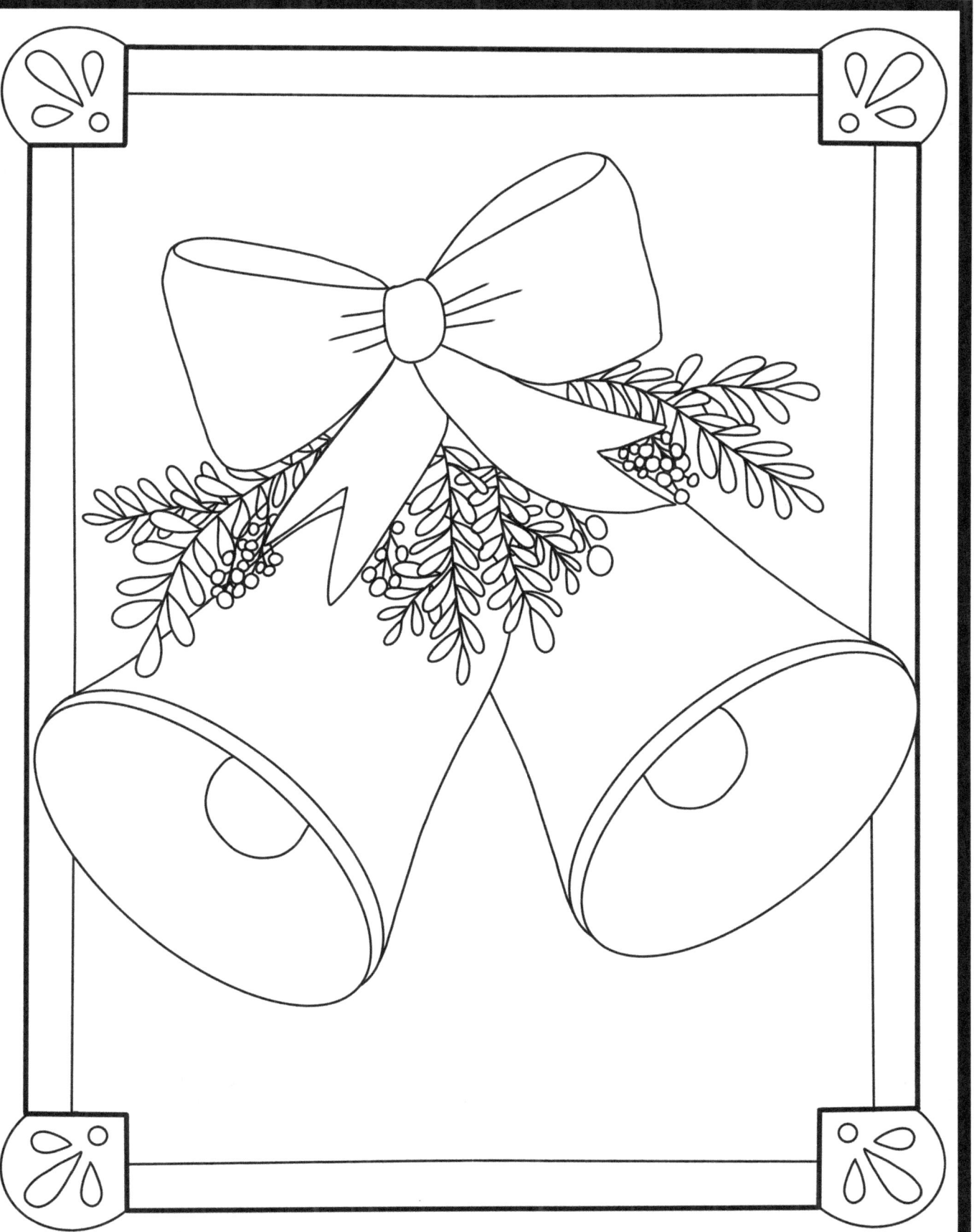

HARK! THE HERALD ANGELS SING

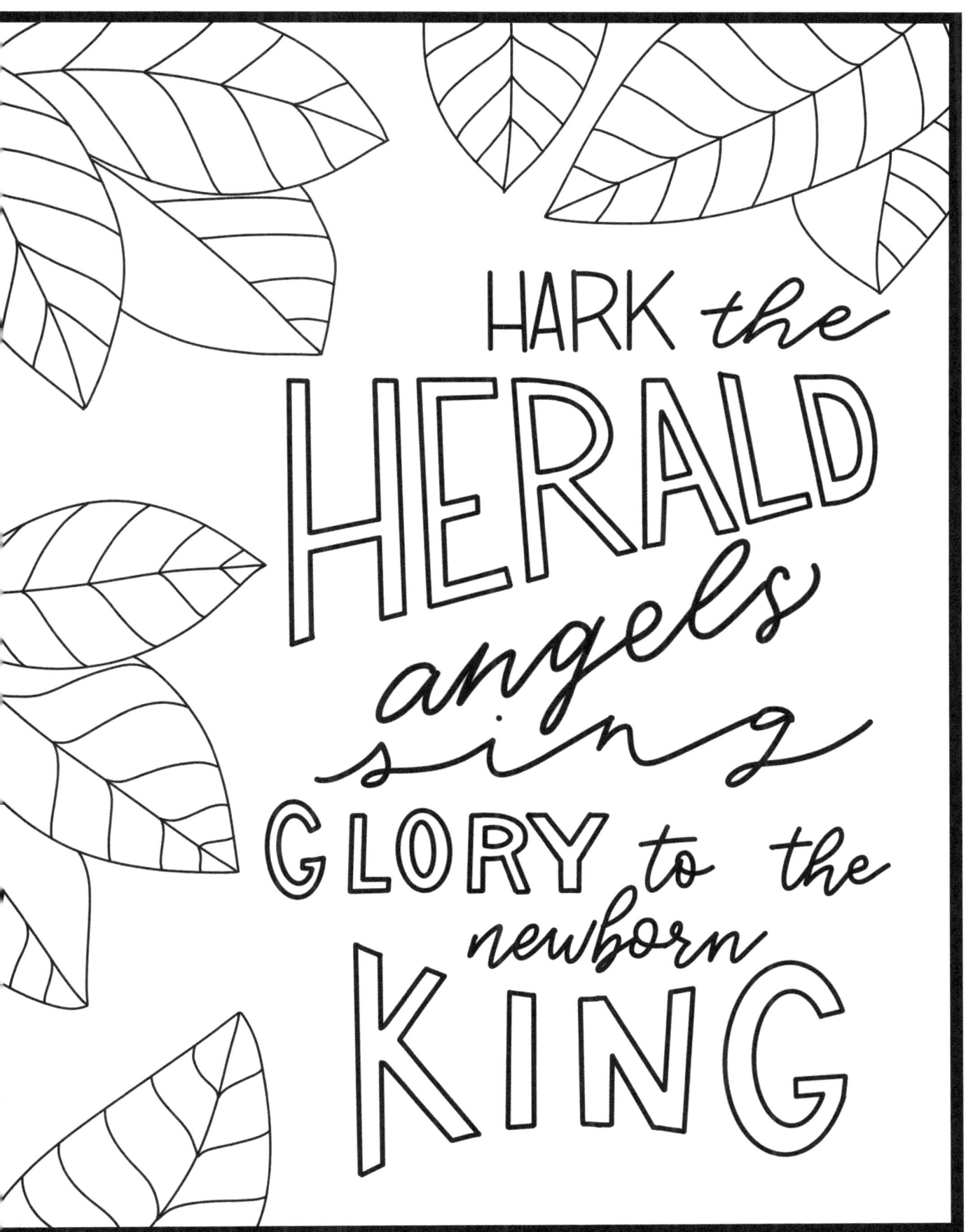

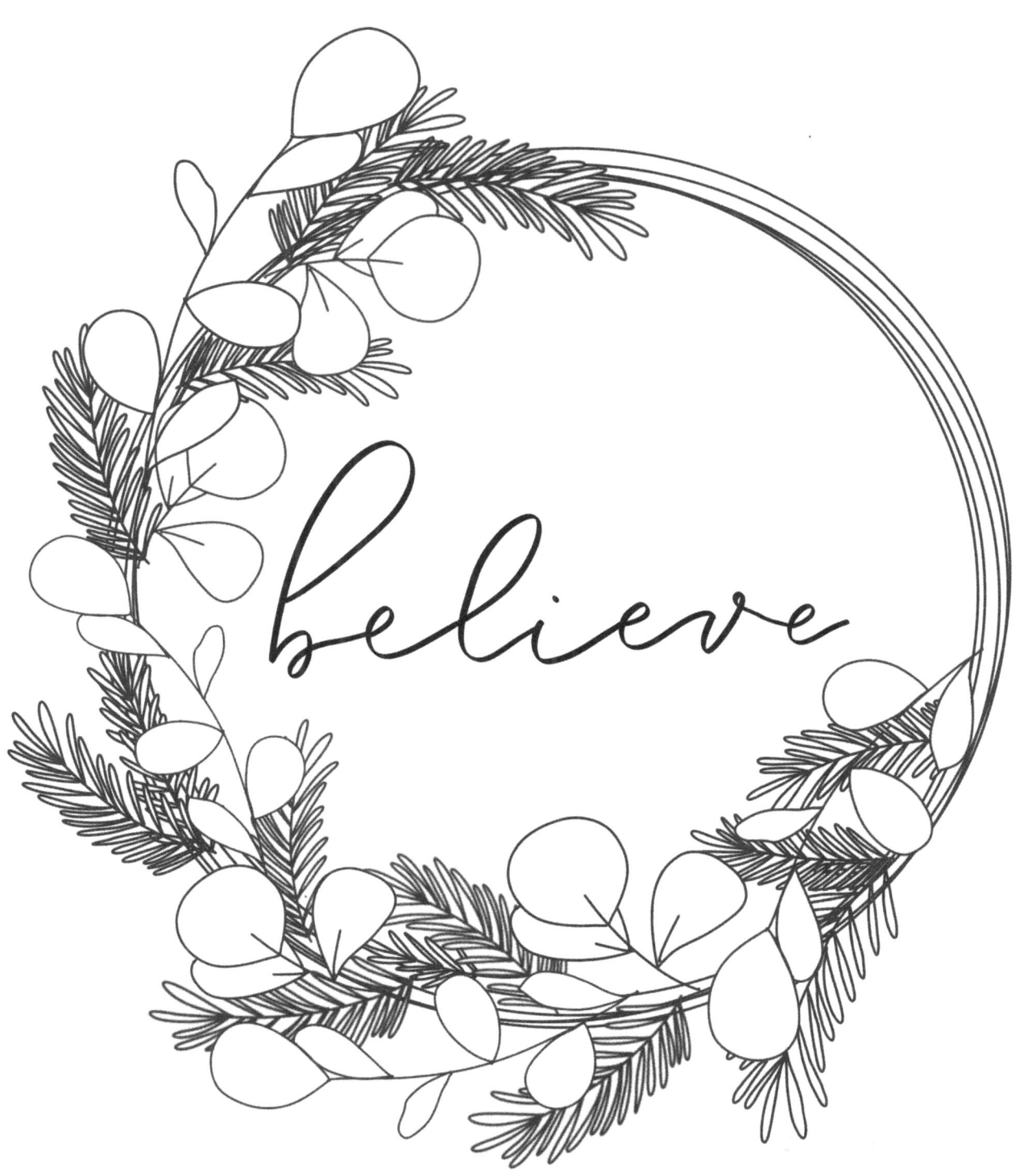

ANGELS WE HAVE HEARD ON HIGH

come adore on bended knee CHRIST the Lord the Newborn KING

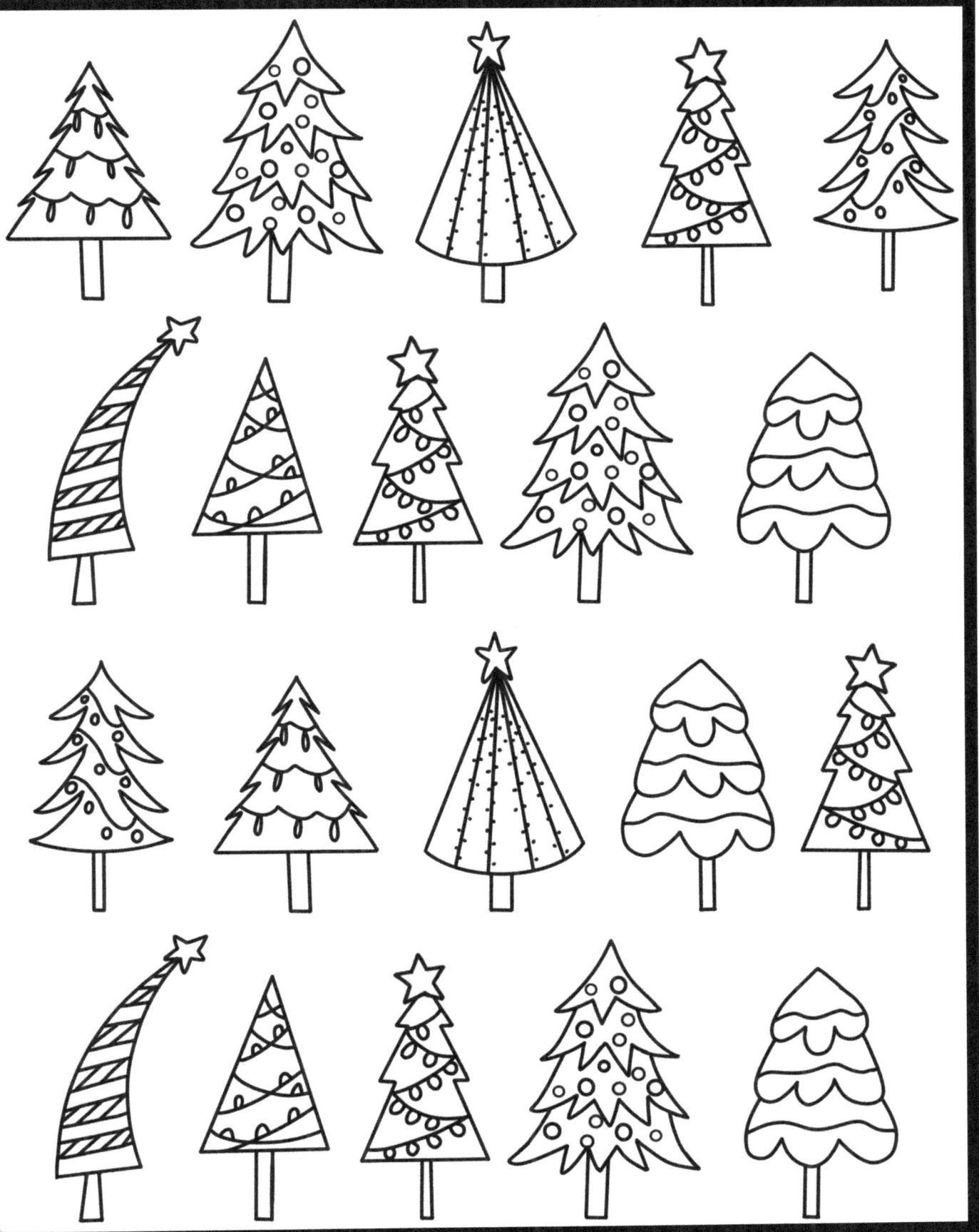

IT CAME UPON THE MIDNIGHT CLEAR

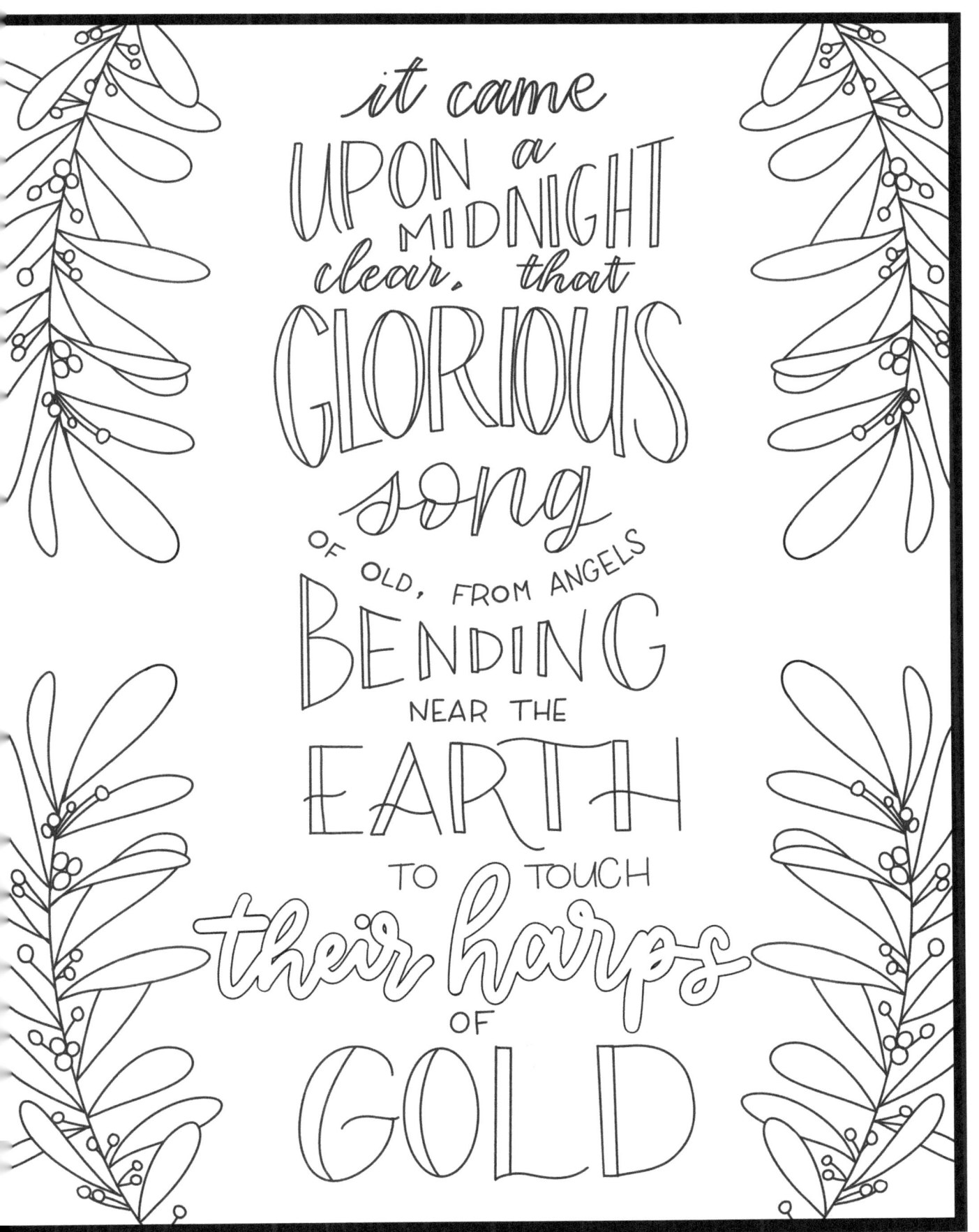

SILENT NIGHT

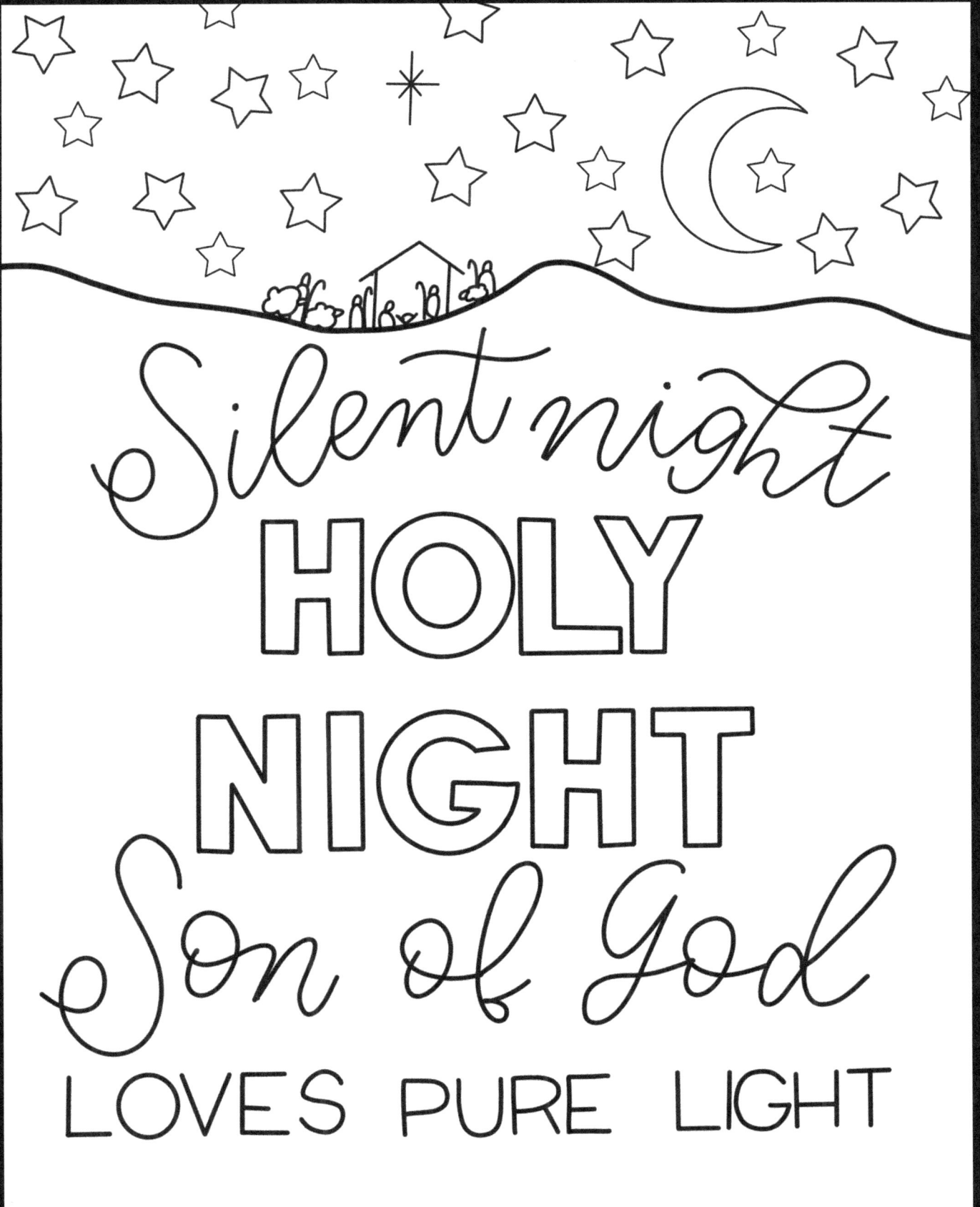

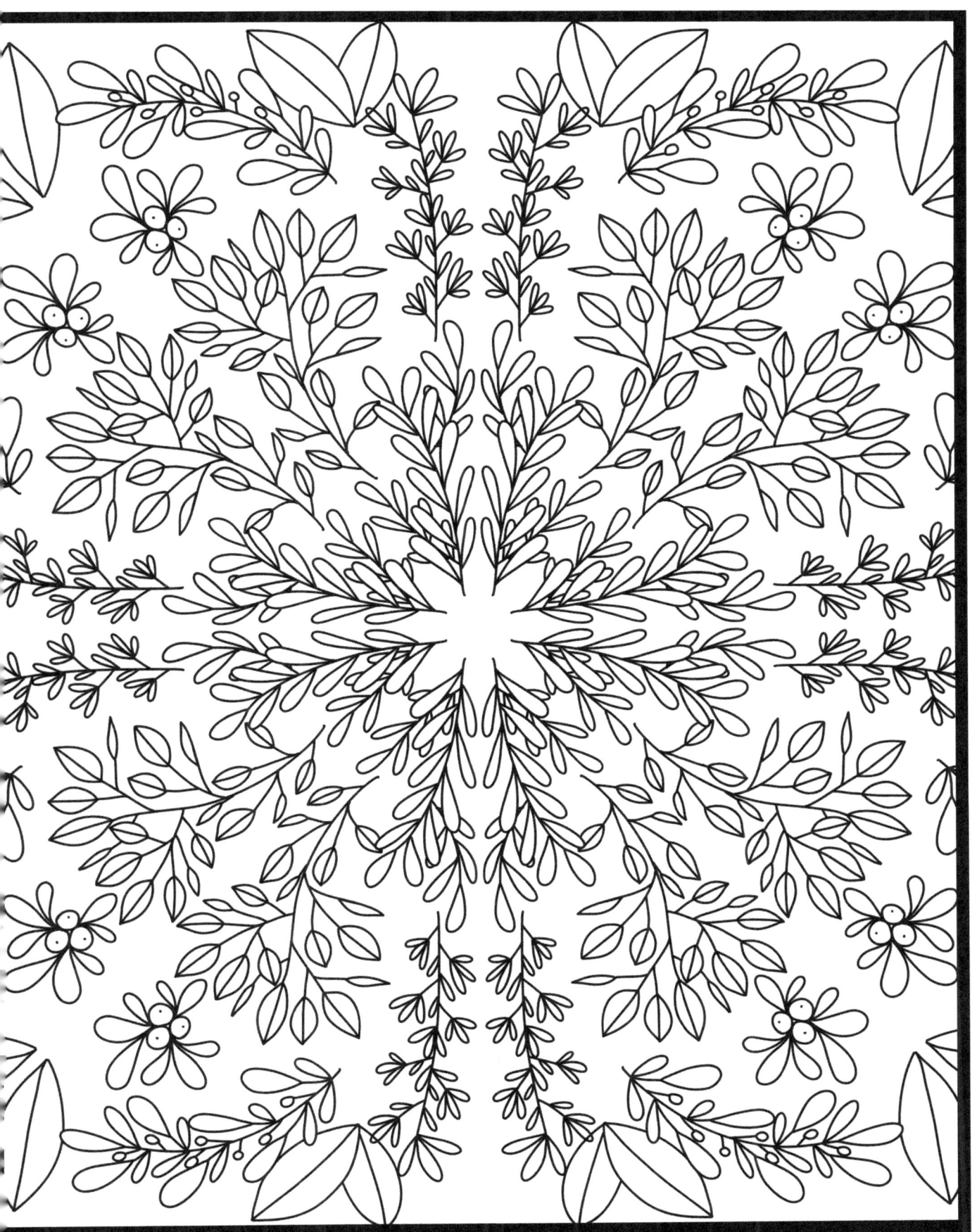

WITH WONDERING AWE

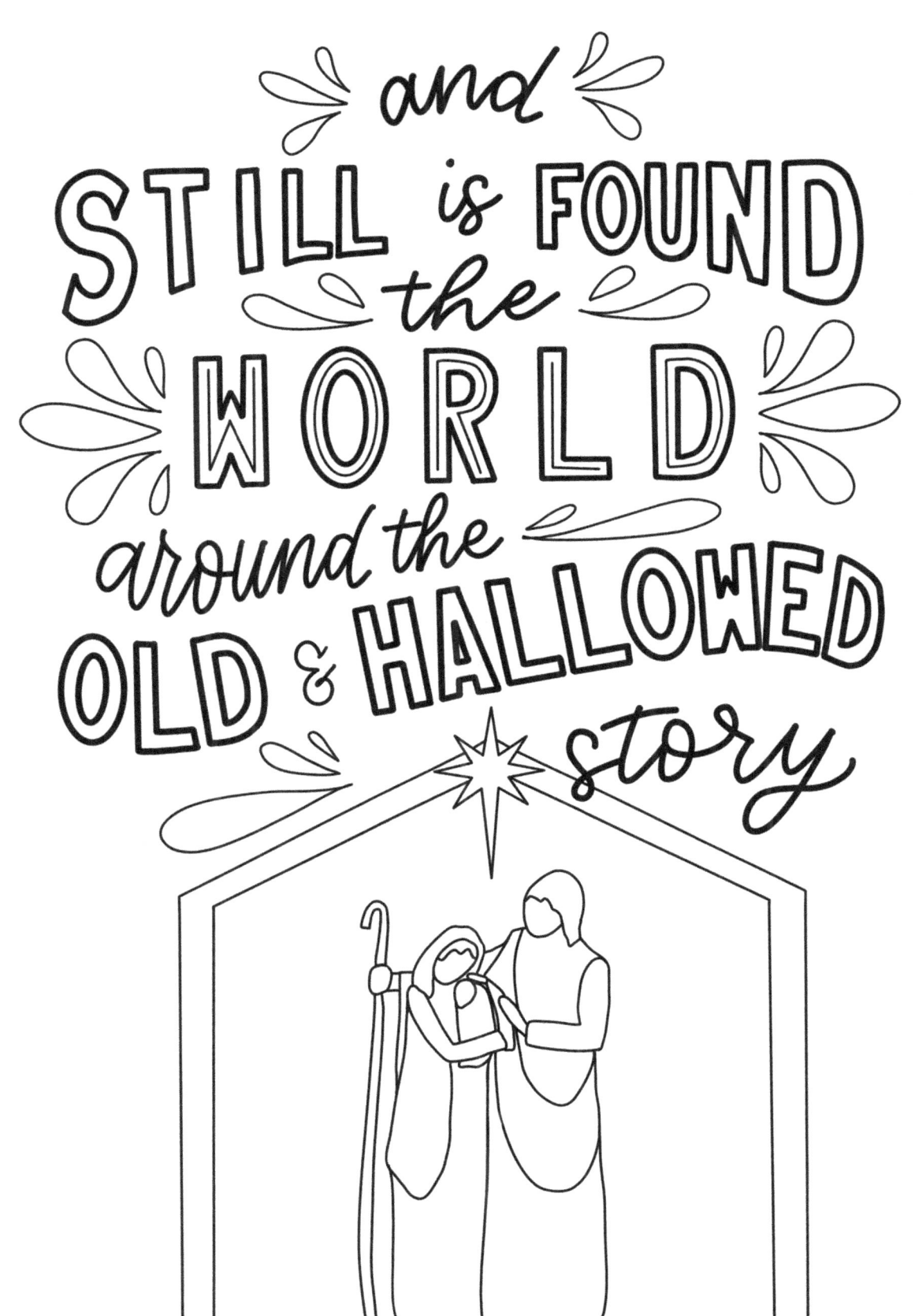